In The Garden

Pamela Rushby

Photography by Alice McBroom

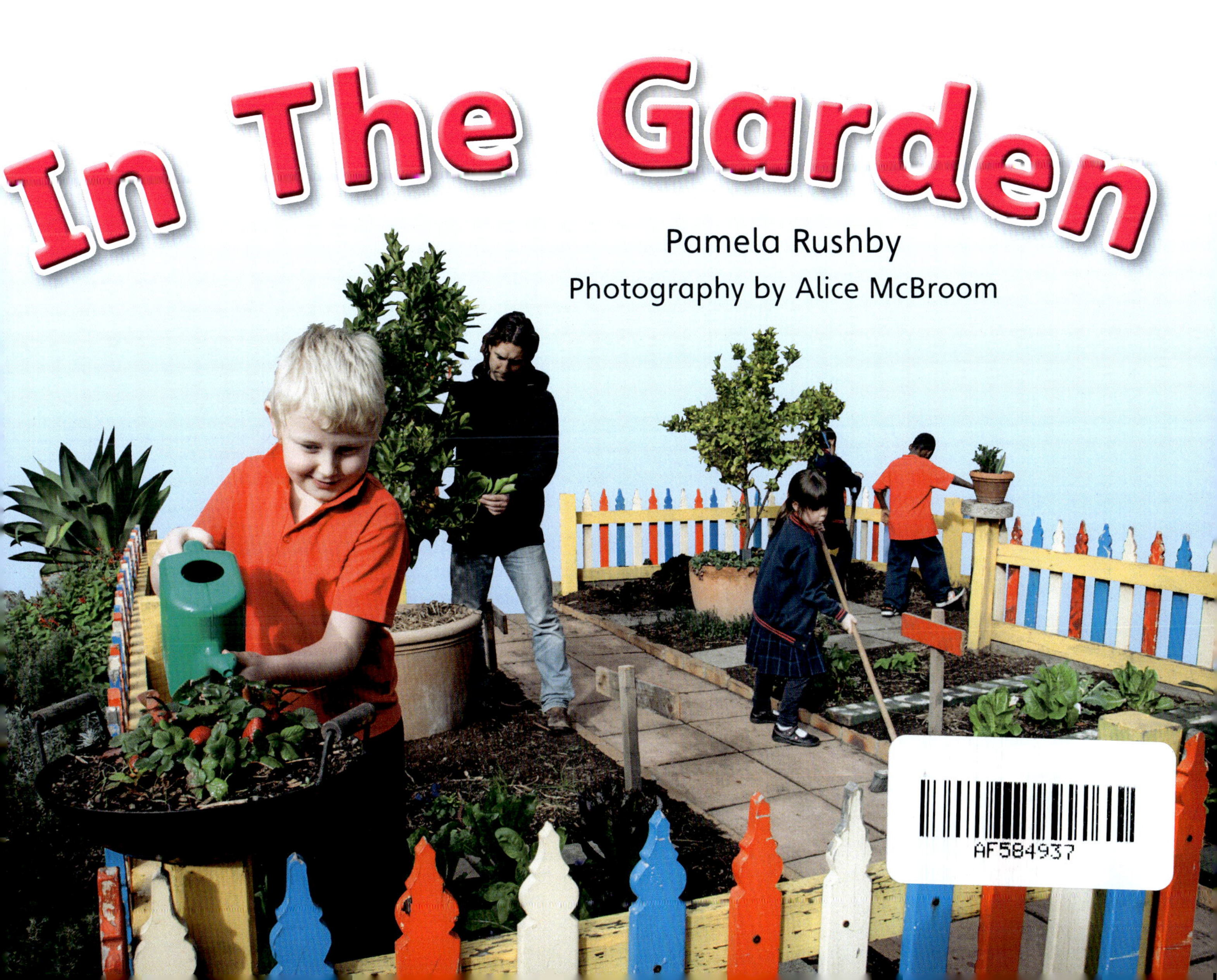

Here is the garden.

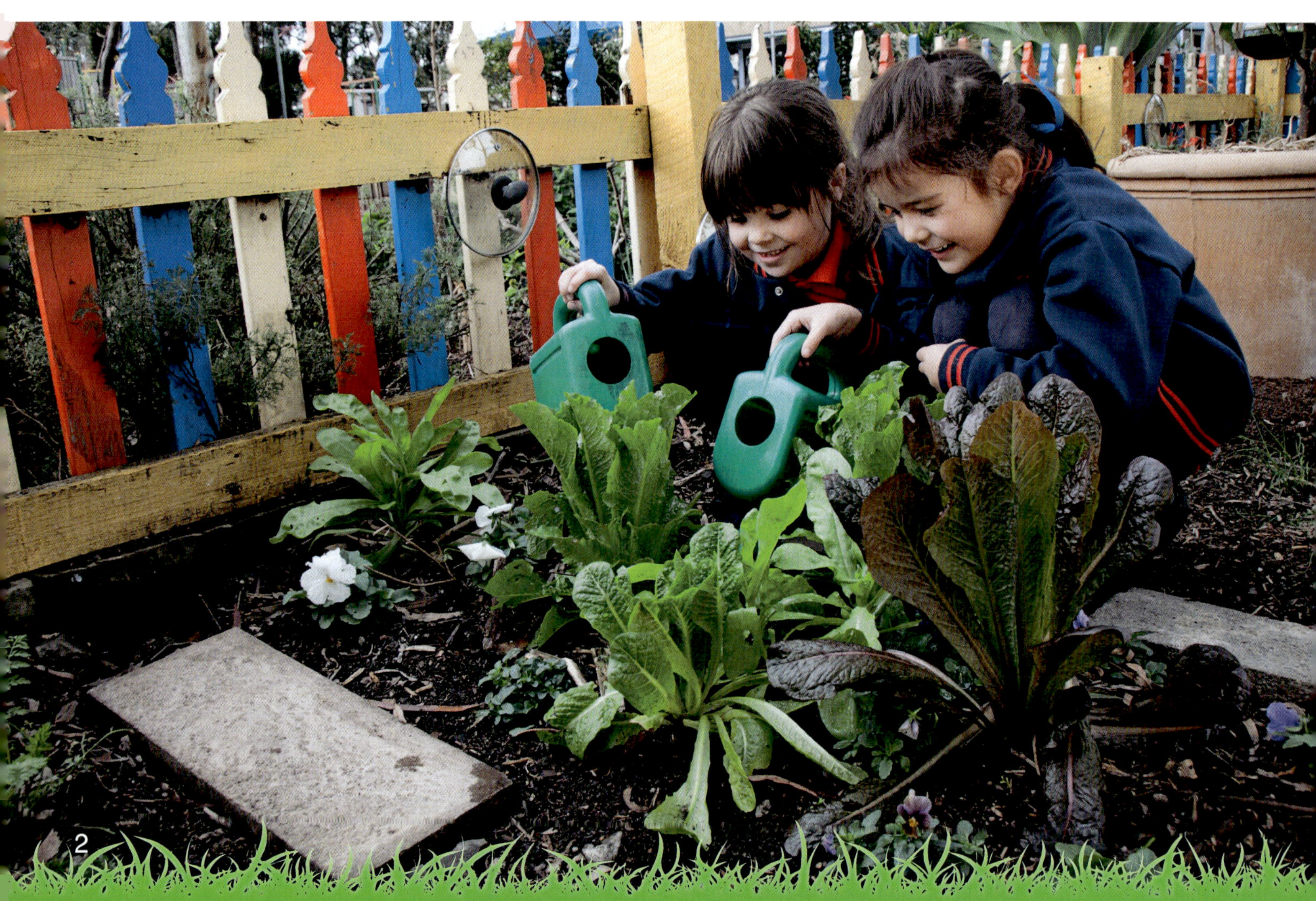

We grow lettuce.

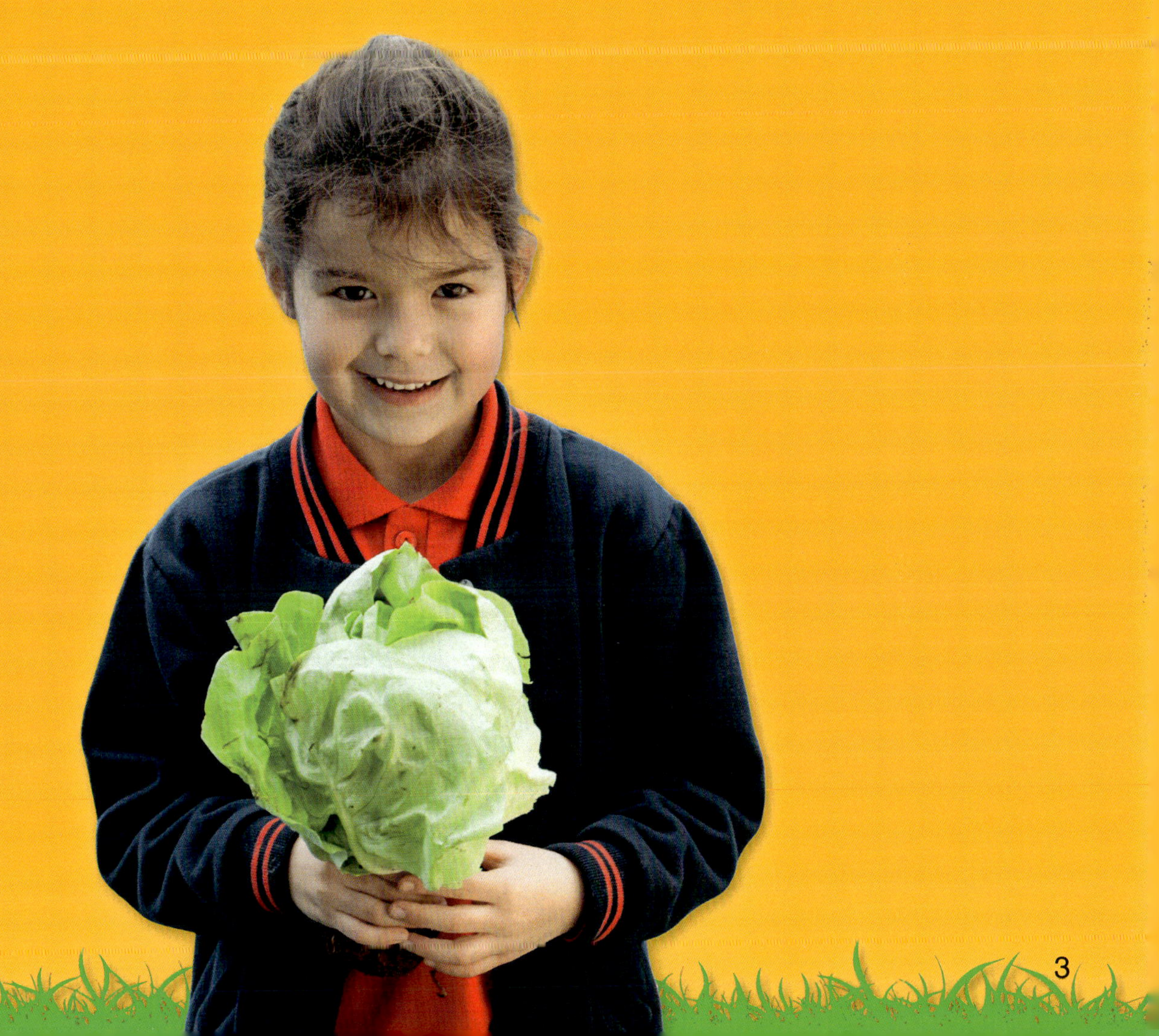

Here is the garden.

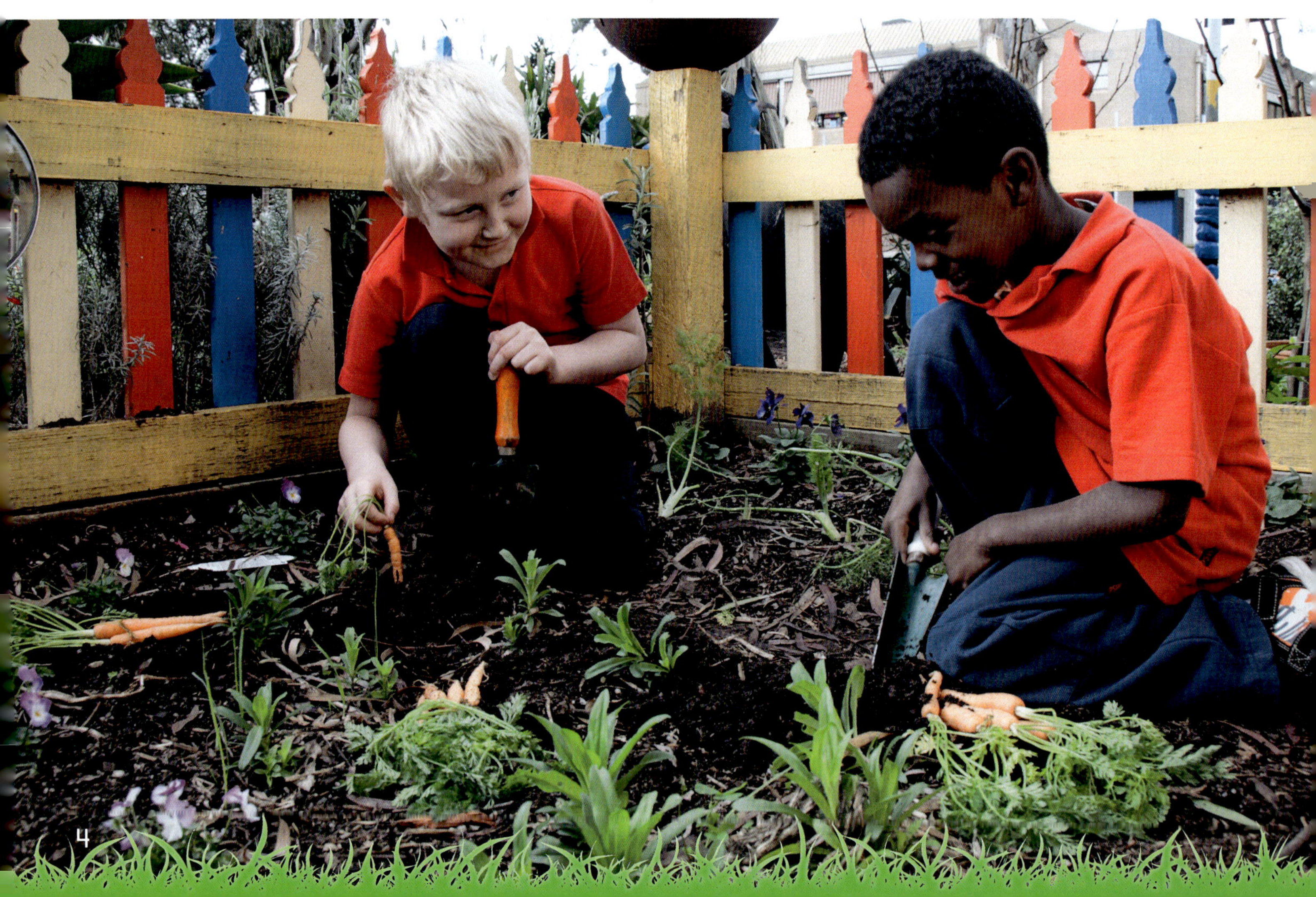

We grow carrots.

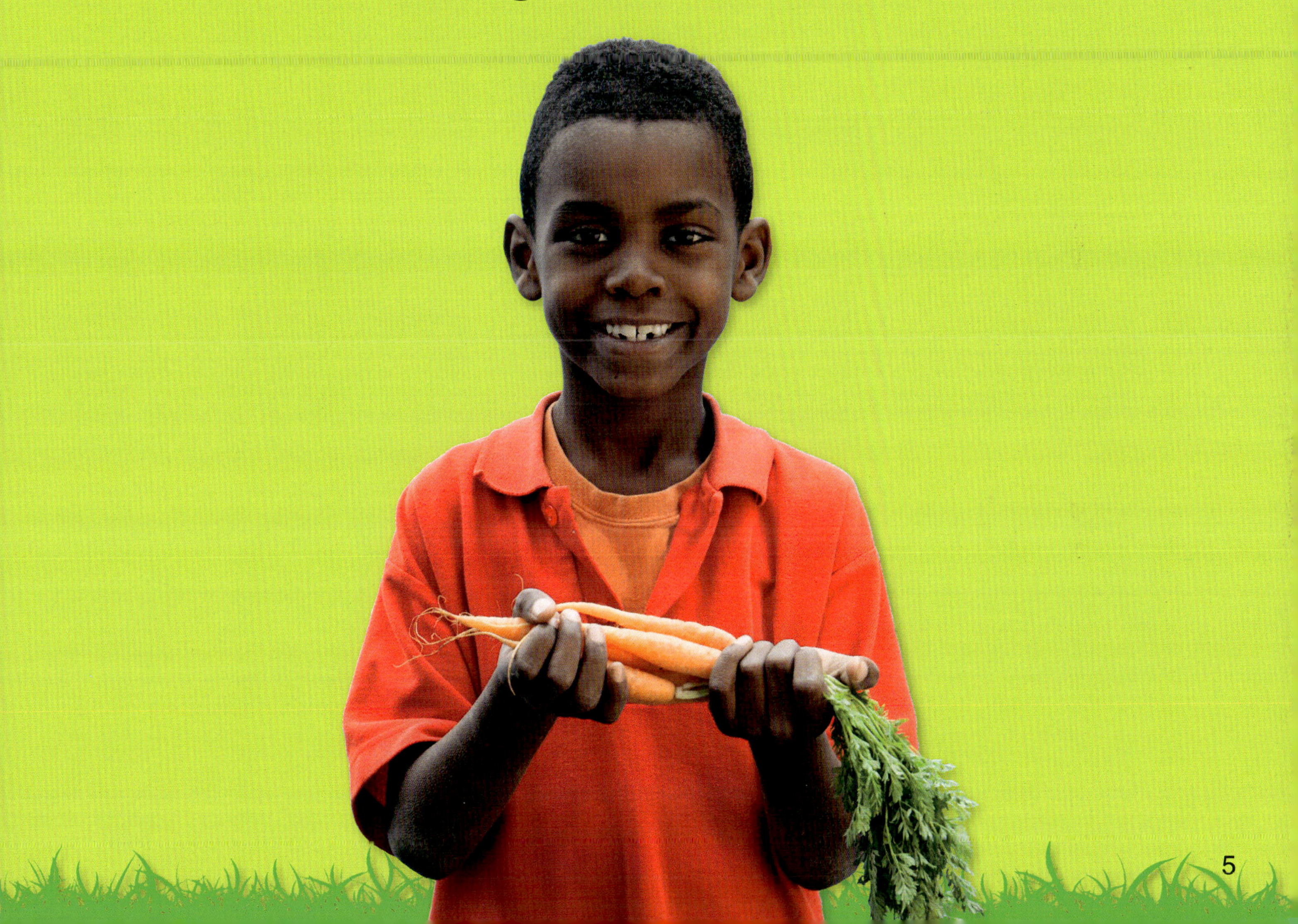

Here is the garden.

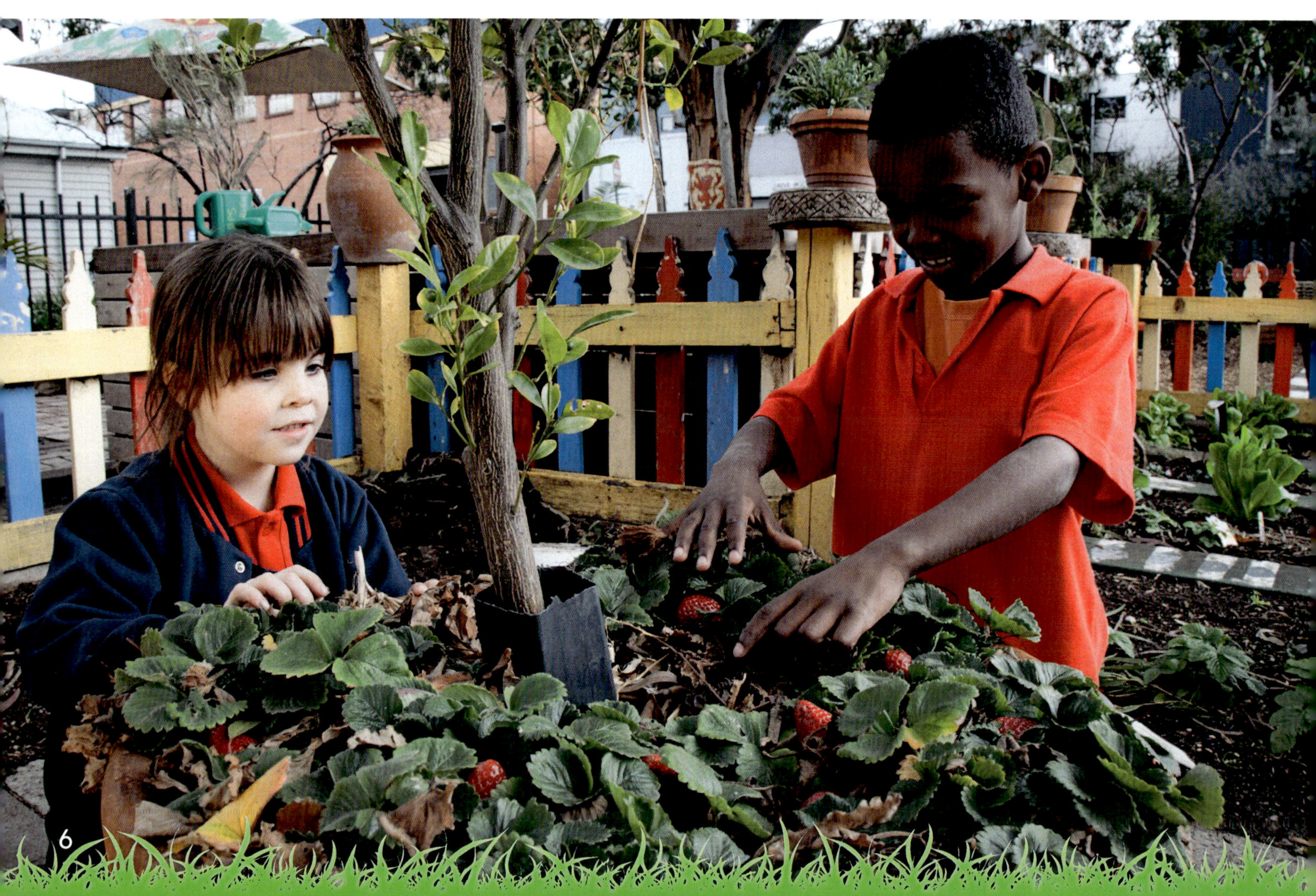

We grow strawberries.

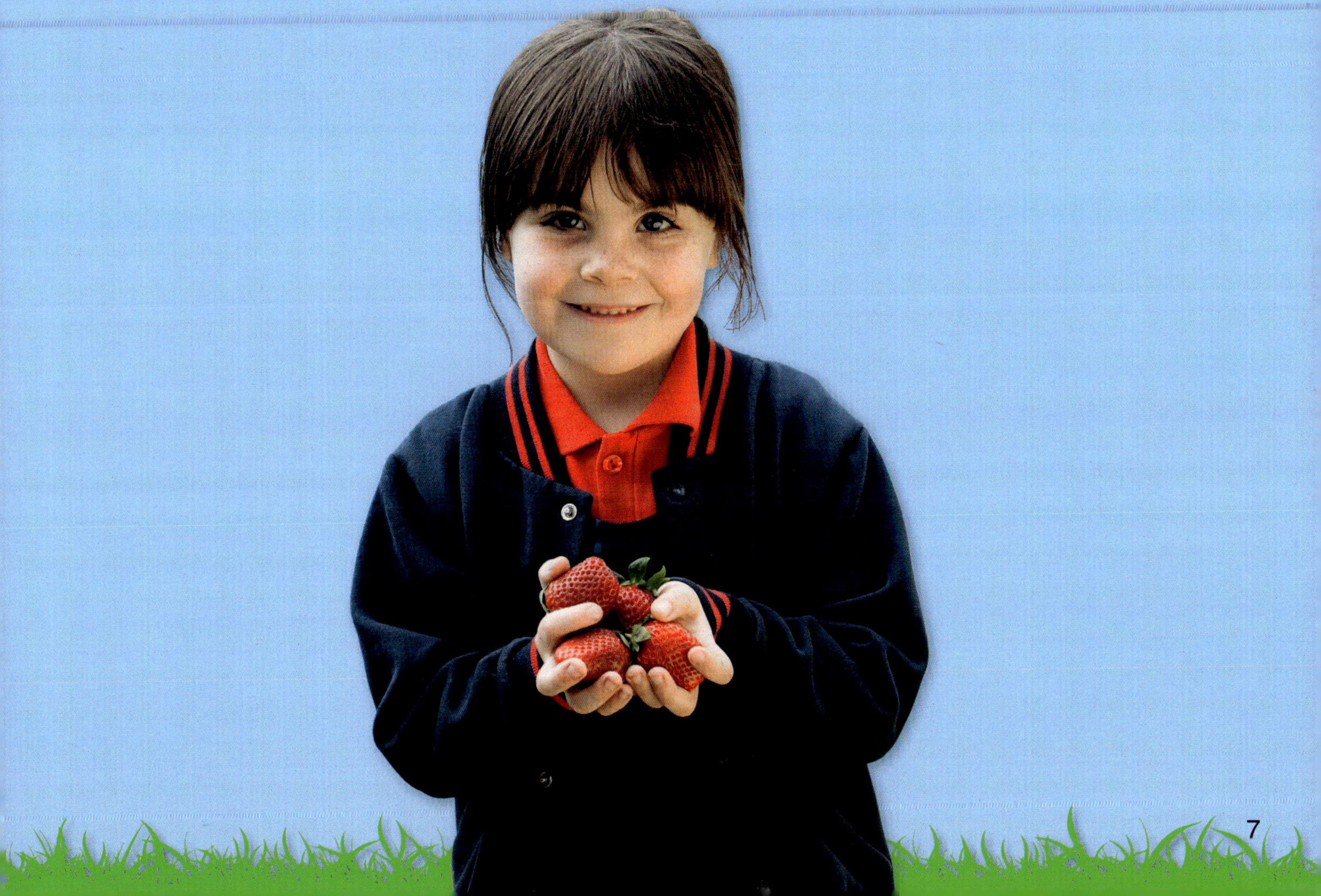

Here is lunch!

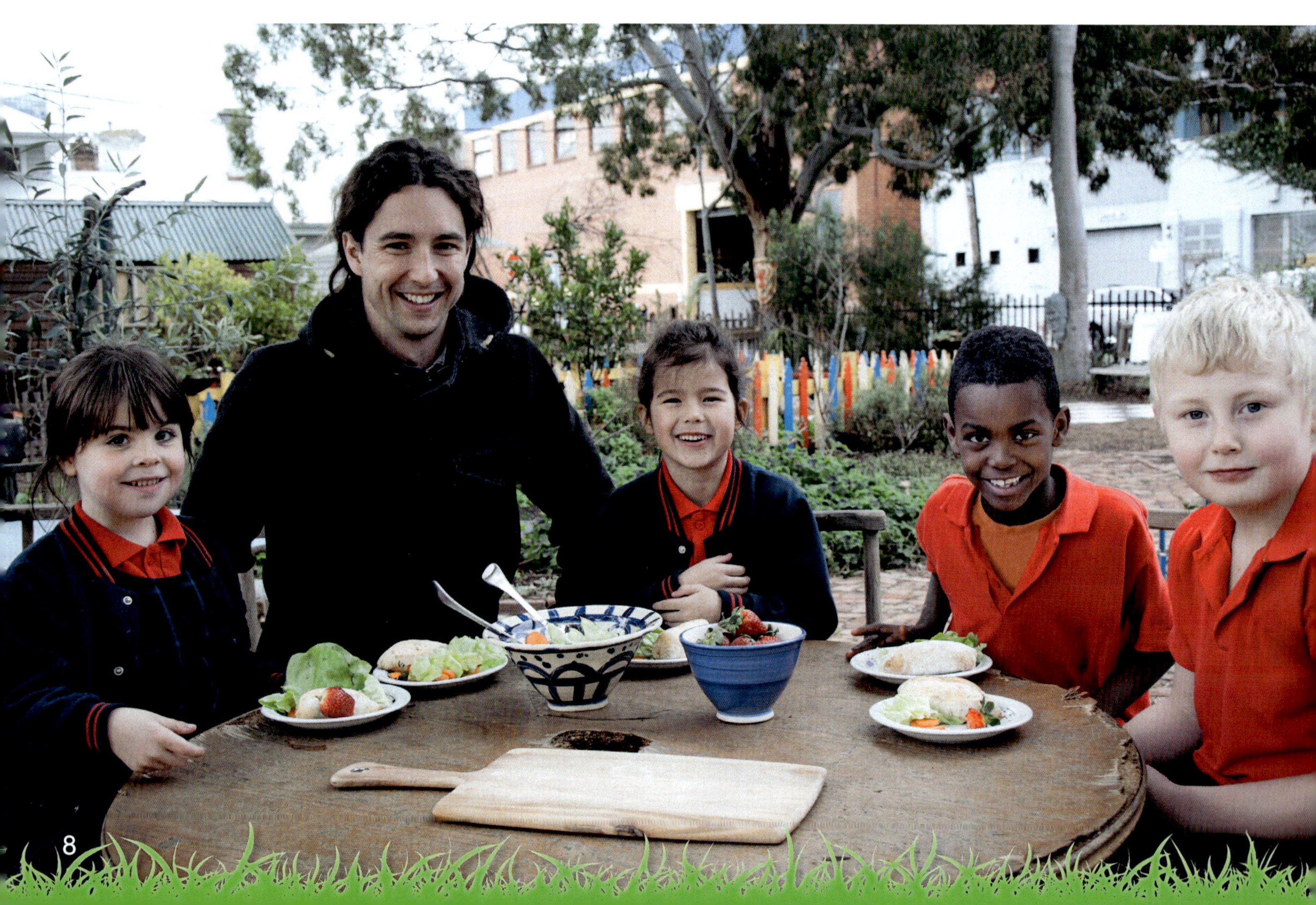